Autism Aspergers: Understanding From The Inside Out

Brad Mason, M.Ed.

Licensed Professional Counselor, Licensed Specialist in School Psychology

Copyright © 2015 Brad Mason, LPC, LSSP

All rights reserved.

ISBN: 1512243027
ISBN-13: 978-1512243024

DEDICATION

This book is dedicated to all those who have suffered needlessly due to misunderstanding, ignorance, and fear.

Autism Aspergers: Understanding from the Inside Out

Forward

I read some years ago in my NASP (National Association of School Psychologists) handbook that "autism is a lifelong disease. " I think this is misleading from two standpoints. First, it's not a disease. It doesn't get worse as time goes on, it doesn't mean the person is sick, and you can't die from it. Second, while there may or may not be a "cure," the symptoms of autism can and usually do improve over time and with effort. Rather than viewing autism as a disease, I would encourage you to think of it as a difference that may at times cause some "dis-ease," and at other times may produce miracles of innovation and creativity.

I made this book for you. I wrote this to spread understanding, acceptance, and appropriate assistance for all the people who have symptoms of autism or asperger syndrome. I have observed and interviewed some special people who have overcome a great many challenges, with help and special

Autism Aspergers: Understanding from the Inside Out

parenting, to find themselves comfortable with who they are and reconciled with the criticisms and judgements they received from others. I want you to become that person for someone else that always has compassion, always thinks well of them, continues to encourage and support even when unexpected behaviors are occurring. Hopefully you had at least one person in your life who you knew always saw you that way, and helped you see yourself as good, lifted you to your better possible self.

I think God made people different for a reason. Look at Einstein and Edison, DaVinci and Mozart.

Who do you think came up with and designed rockets and computers, anyway?

Either you or someone you know has autism. I hope this will help you expand your limits and overcome obstacles. You have no idea how much you have to offer and how far you and those you love can go until you stop limiting. With understanding, love, and therapeutic social connections we can all transform and leap into a happy, healthy, and purposeful life. I've seen this happen over and over in my practice.

This is not intended to be the be-all end-all manual for autism and asperger syndrome, it is meant to give a quick overview that explains why people with this condition have the difficulties and unexpected behaviors they display, and some resources and techniques for getting started on making it better. You should come away with an overview of the characteristics of autism spectrum disorder and have some practical strategies and good resources to help you remediate or compensate for these difficulties and help those on the spectrum do what is expected more often and enjoy a higher quality of life. You can also find an 88 minute video that goes with this book and additional resources at www.icyouvideo.com.

Autism Aspergers: Understanding from the Inside Out

Table of Contents

Page #

9	Mindblindness- Theory of Mind
22	High Anxiety & Stress
28	Bullying
36	Executive Functions
51	Communication
57	Sensory Issues
61	Student Interviews- What's hard, What Helped?
63	Functional implications: Disrupted Sensory Processing
64	Self-esteem
67	Tunnel vision
68	Social Skills
71	Problem Solving
72	Comorbid Mood Disorder
73	Extreme Emotional Response
76	Defense Mechanisms
78	Concluding Comments
83	Resources- Books, Research, Games

93   Appendix- Why Autism?
         Signs of Asperger Syndrome
         Autism Sensitivity Training Resources

Autism Aspergers: Understanding from the Inside Out

Mindblindness- Theory of Mind

Theory of mind, or TOM, means understanding that other people have their own agendas, feelings, and ideas that are separate from yours- their own mind with different plans, opinions, preferences, and experiences. So someone with disruptions in the development of TOM may tend to view the world as if we are all participating in the same stream of consciousness- theirs. This explains why a person on the spectrum may start a conversation somewhere in the middle without providing an introduction or context. Why they might be upset if your plan or opinion differs from theirs. Why they might at times treat others as if they should perform their will as if the separate person were an extension of the spectrum person's body, like one of their hands. Wouldn't you be frustrated if one of your arms or legs suddenly quit working and wouldn't follow your instructions?

On the milder end we may have insistence that an opinion is a fact, neglecting to ask for help (because they don't think about the fact that others may know things they don't) and trouble with perspective-taking. On the severe end of disrupted development of TOM we could have a person who doesn't recognize others as beings to interact with at all.

Characteristics of poorly developed theory of mind could include difficulty with the following;

-*literal*- Concrete and fail to interpret figures of speech/idioms, tend to split hairs such as arguing that it is not 4:00 yet it's only 3:58.

-*empathy*- May not notice how others are feeling or may not modify their behavior to keep others feeling good.

-*perspective taking*- May stay stuck in their perspective and insist others are wrong if they don't agree, may even try to make others agree they are right.

-*persuading*- May demand and insist rather than using tact and diplomacy to influence others.

-*compromise*- Exactly my way or the highway.

Autism Aspergers: Understanding from the Inside Out

-honest to a fault- How much food did you have to eat to get that fat?

-conflict resolution- Lacking diplomacy and tact needed for resolving interpersonal problems.

-get overwhelmed- being around others because they are working so hard to figure them out rather than using intuition.

You may also notice the following characteristics:

-not know when to be embarrassed

-have trouble predicting how others will feel or react to them

-may appear rude and disrespectful

-may be paranoid because others seem so unpredictable

-trouble understanding deception

-starting in the middle of a conversation- think you know what they know

-don't realize or read the cues that others aren't interested in monologues

What are some ways to help a person develop better perspective-taking skills, more empathy, greater consideration of how they impact and shape the experience and feelings of the people with whom they share space?

To help with being overly literal and splitting hairs, I like to teach the kids what splitting hairs means, have them think about trying to split a hair, and show them on a clock with hands and numbers the difference between 3:58 and 4:00, and encourage the parents to use these keywords and anchoring experiences when their kid is "making a mountain out of a molehill" again. It can be fun to conjure and draw images to go with idioms for fun- a "brook chuckling over it's stoney bed," "hurting like fire," "can we get on the same page here?" After laughing we can think about what does this phrase REALLY mean? Apples to Apples is a game that makes you look at how unidentical terms could be somewhat the same, even though not exactly so.

Autism Aspergers: Understanding from the Inside Out

More importantly you can ask kids to make inferences based on nonverbal clues as to what a person's plan might be. For instance, if two people are talking, standing close to one another, and a third person approaches and stands closely watching them but not speaking, what is the silent person's intention? That's right, they want to say or ask something, they are using their body position to give the speaking people awareness that they want something from them without verbally interrupting. You can watch for these teachable moments while at home or in the community, and you can use cartoons as well, pausing on a character before they speak or do something, and asking the child to use the clues to guess what the character is thinking or feeling.

Getting someone with a literal thinking style to make guesses can be tough because many of these folks do not like gray areas- and you can't REALLY know what someone is thinking or planning but you are expected to make a guess or ask if you are not sure. Socializing is really based on a lot of guesswork, much of which you can't be completely sure of.

Most of us do it automatically without thinking about it, but without this guesswork and scaffolding of assumptions, we really can't socialize effectively at all. You have to be willing and able to watch people and make guesses about their thoughts, feelings, and intentions.

You are a Social Detective is a good book to teach younger children- from developmental age of about 4-8 years- how to use what they see and hear to do what is expected and how doing what is unexpected can impact how others feel about them in a negative way.

I also teach kids to defer, which means to allow other people to think they are right even when you think they are wrong- just let it go and don't continue to insist or argue. Sometimes it's better to allow someone to think they are right even though you don't agree so the play or conversation can move forward. Getting someone who is not in the habit of thinking about how others are thinking about them and modifying their behavior to keep others having good thoughts about them will often take

Autism Aspergers: Understanding from the Inside Out

many, many repeated trials. Using behavior modification techniques to increase motivation will help too. (How would this look? Please see my video <u>Behavior Management at it's Best</u>, and take some valuable concepts and techniques that can help you every day).

For greater grasp of deception I like to give kids in my groups some real money and teach them to play poker. I explain bluffing, ways to recognize a bluff and how to manage your nonverbal communication to make a bluff, and I explain that people out there in the world will try to deceive you to get your money. There are also some games you can play with them, such as <u>Fib or Not</u> and <u>Fact or Crap.</u> In <u>Fib or Not</u> the kids have to either tell a story that is true but try to convince their playmates the story is a lie, or they have to tell a story that is a lie but convince playmates it is true.

Another concept related to being literal or black and white with interpretations of honesty is the "social fake." Many of the kids and young adults I have worked with are extremely uncomfortable with not being genuine and honest. You may be thinking right now, what's wrong with being genuine and honest? Consider these social scenarios. Your best friend enters with a new haircut, and you think it looks terrible on them. How do you know if it's okay to be honest? Would it ever be a better choice to lie or try to say something nice about their appearance? How do you judge with whom and when you tell the truth and when you, well, massage the truth a little bit? You consider what you know about the person based on past experience and try to predict their reaction, and weigh you options carefully. Here's another example of the social fake. You're at a party and you are introduced to someone new. You are not sure if you really want to meet them or if you will like them. If you convey your uncertainty and doubt with your body language, you may cross your arms, hold yourself at a greater distance from them, and look away from them more than what is expected. How will they interpret your behavior? (This person doesn't like me or want to talk to me.) So it's better to pretend, with your posture, tone, and words, by making eye contact, smiling, and pretending to be

Autism Aspergers: Understanding from the Inside Out

happy and interested. This is expected! Doing something unexpected will likely cause them to have weird or uncomfortable thoughts about you. Act happy and interested, and you may "fake it until you make it." You will either find some common ground and interest with the new person and if not, you should make some excuse to excuse yourself, and say something possibly not quite true. "Oh, look, there's Pete, I really need to go talk to him, it was really great meeting you and I hope to see you again!"

A related concept is *central coherence.* Central coherence refers to what is typically a natural process for the mind to take in details and create a meaningful concept that explains how the details fit together to form an idea. What happens if a mind memorizes or just perceives details without trying to make meaning and link pieces together to draw conclusions? You get trouble with big picture thinking, reading comprehension, understanding and predicting the behavior and intentions of others.

Soooo... how else can you help someone develop this ability? Ask questions while reading to a child such as "What is this about?" "What do you think will happen next?" "How do you think the characters are thinking/feeling?" "How will they react and what sort of plan might they come up with?" "What is the problem and how could it be solved?" You can do the same thing watching cartoons and movies, you can even pause, and see if the child can guess the feelings as well. You can provide prompts to "get outside their head" to use the eyes, ears, and brain to gather information from the environment, figure out what others are doing, what they expect from others in the same group or space, or how they can help.

There's a book called <u>Teaching Children with Autism to MInd Read</u>. It presents pictures of people in a situation, like a snake in front of a girl, and asks how will she feel, to facilitate predicting others' emotions based on a situation. The next step has pictures and stories where a character's desires are indicated and then they either do or do not get what they want- helping to develop the understanding that people are happy when they get what they want and not happy when they don't. Then they throw a curve in. What if Billy wants a plane for his birthday, but he thinks he is getting a kite, how will he feel then? And when he finds out he is getting a plane after all? So we have predicting others' emotions based on what their beliefs.

Another way to develop perspective taking and big picture thinking is to ask them to guess someone's plan based on an observed action- like if someone has trash in their hand and they are headed for the trash can, what do you think their plan is? What is their intention? One child is swinging and laughing while another is standing close by with clenched fists and crying- why is one crying and what could they want?

Social skills groups can help here too. It makes sense to me to say that some kids may not develop empathy until they have experienced feeling successful having fun with others in a group. If it's more rewarding playing by yourself, why should you care what others think and feel? But when someone discovers how much MORE fun and exciting it can be in a shared experience, then they start to develop some buy-in to working at being with others and caring about their thoughts and feelings.

Some of my favorite and most effective social skills and perspective taking resources come from Michelle Garcia-Winner, www.socialthinking.com, such as the Superflex curriculum, you can see me using some of it in my social skills video. I try to teach social and perspective taking concepts as many ways as I can to try and get the point across- role-play, comic strips, video modeling, charts, stories, coaching in the context of real interactions with other kids. About 15 years ago I was doing a group with kids aged 6-7, and this one really bright dragon-loving girl kept bringing really cool stuff in her backpack to play with before the group would start. The other kids would see it and want to check it out, too, but this little girl would not share. Finally we brought some really cool stuff and took it out and played with it, when she asked to try it out, we

Autism Aspergers: Understanding from the Inside Out

said no, and kept exclaiming how fun it was to play with it. She got mad and asked why, so we explained this was what it was like for the others when she brought out her cool stuff and wouldn't share. The next time we met, she brought out some cool light up toy, the other kids asked if they could see it more closely, she said "NO." Again. We reminded her about her experience the previous meeting and she groaned but then finally shared. She needed to experience for herself what it was like to get the point and modify her behavior.

High Anxiety and Stress

If you had trouble understanding what others expect of you, thought about things differently than those around you, got overwhelmed by your sensory experience of just being in the world, and got repeated messages that you either were doing something wrong or weren't doing what you were supposed to do, you'd get nervous and or mad, too, wouldn't you? Remember we are probably talking about someone who has a history of failure and rejection, tends to be perfectionist and extreme- it's all good or all bad, and they use intellect rather than intuition to figure out social situations so they are working harder and get overwhelmed more easily. I have a whole video for you about anxiety as well as self-esteem.

I would imagine the concept of feelings could be troublesome for some people on the spectrum. Not that I don't think they feel- quite to the contrary, in fact. I believe often they may feel much more and intensely and consequently need to escape others or block themselves from feeling so as to prevent

Autism Aspergers: Understanding from the Inside Out

becoming overwhelmed. The part that is difficult about feeling is... what does anxious feel like? It's not the same for me as it is for you. Emotional arousal is the same across many feelings within the same person as it is different between persons. I think we detect our arousal level, then we use the context to give the feeling a name. I'm watching someone I don't really like drive a car I wish I had, and my body is telling me I'm stressed or worried or mad or something, hmmm, I must be jealous. See what I mean?

Tony Attwood made some good workbooks- <u>Exploring Feelings</u>- one of my favorite parts is that he has a menu to choose from for what your body does when you are having an emotional response- do you get sweaty palms, itchy skin, tight muscles, etc. It also has some cognitive-behavioral strategies for dealing with feelings, like his list of poisonous thoughts and antidotes to poisonous thoughts. For example, "I never do anything right," is a poisonous thought, whereas "Sometimes I make mistakes, but most of the time I get it right, and I can try again or get help" would be an antidote to that poisonous thought. Lastly, I like his "emotional toolbox" idea, with categories of tools you can use to help manage or dissolve anxious feelings:

Social Tools- You can talk to someone you trust.

Thinking Tools- Grade the size of the problem on a scale from 1-10, use your self-talk, think to yourself "that's okay, I can handle it."

Activity Tools- Do something you love, go outside and run until you feel better.

Relaxation tools- guided imagery, breathing, hot bath, meditation

Other tools- special interest, medicine, humor

Inappropriate tools- These are things you may do when worried or stressed, but they don't solve the problem or they make things worse.

The Incredible 1-5 Scale by Buron and Curtis, 1993, is great too, it helps teach gradations- rather than all or nothing, like happy or having a meltdown with no in-between, and develop an emotional vocabulary, if you want to see how I use it... see

Autism Aspergers: Understanding from the Inside Out

my video Anxiety and Children or Anger and Children. By the way, often I find that underneath what looks like anger we have anxiety, anger is the behavior we see that the person is using to make things work the way they want, because they are anxious about deviations from what they want or expect. Find a template for a "1-5 scale" in and many more useful free forms under "Learn More" and then click "Forms4u" on my practice website, www.bradmasoncounselor.com.

I like teaching thinking strategies the best, because they are powerful, portable (you can bring them with you as long as you can remember them) and private (nobody can see you using them). *Your thoughts are so powerful they create your reality.* It's not what happens that creates your feelings, it's how you think about what happens. It could start raining right now, and I could get really mad about it, by thinking, no, it can't be raining, this is going to ruin everything, how will I go fishing now? I could stay mad about it all day. Or, I could get happy about it, I could think, hey, this is great, my grass and garden will grow better, maybe the river will fill up so I can go kayaking! And so I could be happy about the rain all day. Same event in both cases, the rain, different thoughts=different feelings.

For younger children, the book Thotso by Avery, R. (2008) can help you teach how this works. It introduces that idea that your brain can make thoughts that make you smile, and thoughts that hurt- smiling thoughts and boo-boo thoughts. When you have a boo-boo thought, you can make a smiling thought to help yourself feel better. For older kids there is a game called Land of Psymon, it has cards kind of like pokemon cards, representing categories of unwanted or incorrect thoughts, like the Extremist, who tries to make you think if it's not perfect, it's terrible, and smarter ways to think, like the Wish-fish, who reminds you that things are never all good or all bad, we can wish they were perfect and be content with what we get or do.

For adults or teens, we can use cognitive distortions, you will find these categories of thinking errors, sometimes I just call

Autism Aspergers: Understanding from the Inside Out

them stupid ways to think, in Forms4u, located under "Learn More," the document is called "Cognitive Distortions."

You will also find in Forms4u a menu of "Stress Triggers," "Stress Signs," and "Stress Management Strategies." Have the child you are caring for highlight the items from the menu that resonate with them. Use this to identify triggers and possibly eliminate them from the environment, help them develop greater awareness of when they are getting stressed before it's too late and they start acting out, and to have a menu of strategies for managing their emotional responses or care for themselves in appropriate ways.

There are also lifestyle adjustments you can make, preventative measures to keep stress at bay, such as exercise, daily nap, meditation, or prayer, eating healthy, avoidance or reduction of stress triggers, spending time having fun, downtime scheduled, time with friends, regular sleeping habits.

Bullying

By middle school if not earlier humans in our culture, for whatever reason, begin to fear and sometimes target and criticize anyone who is different, even if the differences are small such as skin tone, how your voice sounds, the structure of your facial features, or how your hair is cut and groomed. These nuances of appearance and behavior, and the rejection of an individual who looks or sounds different, make up what we call culture, and establish how we identify someone as a member of our group, or tribe, and one who is not a member, or an outcast. Being an outcast and not having a group to identify with for protection is threatening. For one, outcast or non-member status invites the possibility of attack from groups or tribes that strike out at non-members as a way to defend territory and resources.

And human beings are fragile. We are born vulnerable, unable to survive alone, dependent on the goodwill and care of others for our survival. Even as adults most of us would have

Autism Aspergers: Understanding from the Inside Out

difficulty surviving in the wilderness alone. We live in groups with rules called civilization for this reason. We specialize- we find our way to contribute to others, services that are needed or wanted, that we can provide to other group members in exchange for goods and services we may want or need for ourselves. Most of us don't know how to make the shoes we wear, the roof over our head, the food for our table, how to make medicine or provide defense against attackers or birth babies. We each do our thing so we can get someone else to do the things we don't have the skills or training for. This is how we live. Nearly everything we get or enjoy is derived from relationship; our status with others is important and helps give value to what we can do for others in exchange for what we need.

Unfortunately I have seen kids who were bullied mercilessly at school by the same kids year after year. Add to that the way some kids on the spectrum can hold a grudge, focusing on one negative and ignoring all other positives in their life, and the way they can have a friend who does them wrong one time and suddenly they are the enemy and there is no flexibility for forgiveness,.

Bullying is a natural way to establish dominance and gain favor with peers. When the dominant member of a group, or a member trying to curry favor with the rest of the group and elevate their own status, can put down, ridicule or ostracize someone else, they are actually augmenting their position in the social hierarchy. So some bullying is a fairly common behavior exhibited by popular kids.

What to do? For one thing, you can normalize it- a little teasing is normal, not something to freak out about, sometimes it's just good natured ribbing, this is, after all, the way a lot of grown up men talk to each other all the time. There is a website where you can purchase useful materials, and get some free, to help with bullying. It's at bullies2buddies.com and it focuses treatment on the victim rather than the perpetrator.

Autism Aspergers: Understanding from the Inside Out

My sister-in-law, Jen Mason, who teaches self-defense at a university in Minneapolis, says they prefer the word "target" instead of "victim" because the implied powerlessness is removed, and they use the word "offender," instead of "perpetrator."

The creator of bullies2buddies, Izzy Kalman, says that programs that focus on the perp don't work- think about it, the school punishes the bully, and guess what, the idea that you cause discomfort for someone less powerful than you is reinforced. They get out of in-school suspension and go right out and do it again. He teaches six rules to follow including refuse to let the other person make you upset, treat the words of everyone as if they are words from your best friend. Don't fight back, if you are hurt then say it. He teaches that bullying is all about winning and losing, that if you stay calm and in control, you look like the winner and the bully ends of looking like a jerk. A couple sentences don't do his program justice, it's a good program and is part of what I use in my clinic. Most of the kids on the spectrum who come to my clinic have had trouble with bullying, many are to the point that they are refusing to go back to their school, often their reactions to bullying are getting them into trouble.

You can help by teaching them to discriminate between less harmful teasing and when they are truly being hurt or exploited- laughed at or laughed with? Is this coming from someone who usually treats you well? You can check it out with them- "Are you seriously trying to put me down and hurt me or are you just joking around?"

Telling a teacher is not always the best answer. It can backfire when the accused bully gets in trouble and takes revenge and when other students disrespect the tattle tale. If you fight back, even if you get in trouble or get beat up, at least you may stop the problem and earn respect- from others and for yourself. Sometimes fighting back, while not the school's solution, is a better solution socially. If it was my kid, and they had been bullied by the same person, tattled to school staff, and the bullying kept happening, I'd tell them- I have five boys, one on the spectrum, and have told them this- next time they try to hurt you, either punch them hard right in the nose or kick them in the balls. You will get in trouble at school but not at home. My kids liked being given this option but none of them have used it yet- I think they just preferred to not show a big reaction or make a big deal out of it and the bully moved on to more reactive targets.

It can be really hard to ascertain remotely whether your kid is really being put down or they are being included in the normal jocular banter that occupy the hallways of public schools in Texas. It's good to have something to say back if you are in front of peers and you want to preserve your pride.

Zingers and comebacks for verbal abuse and put-downs:
You would say that.
Wow, you really know how to hurt me.
Does trying to hurt me make you feel better about yourself?
If you put me down do your so-called friends like you better?

I'm sorry for you if your friends and parents talk to you that way.

Okay and by the way go ahead and offer whatever criticism you like, because I've already decided nothing you can say can hurt me.

I know you are, but what am I?

I'm rubber and you're glue, whatever you say bounces off of me and sticks to you.

Remember one of the ways we can make ourselves less of an easy target is to walk with a confident gait and appear switched on and aware of our surroundings.

I know, some of these possible responses are risky and may be controversial. It's a risky and controversial world we live in. I think you need to use your best judgement and discretion if you are coaching a child in ways to respond to bullying.

Often the neurotypical kids are better at being sneaky, provoke the kids on the spectrum, and the kid being bullied gets in trouble for retaliating. The whole crowded noisy public

Autism Aspergers: Understanding from the Inside Out

school scene doesn't work out well anyway, for some kids with autism. You can also look for a small charter or private school.

Executive Functions

Executive functions, or executive skills, are brain skills. These brain skills originate from the frontal lobe of the brain, which is if you will the conductor of the orchestra of our behavior. This is the last part of the brain to develop in a fetus, so any disruption such as premature birth may result in this are of the brain failing to develop on the expected developmental timetable. You might say that milder disruptions in executive functions may result in ADHD, and more significant disruptions may result in Autism Spectrum Disorder. It is also worthy to note that when a fetus turns male, a wash of testosterone kills many brain cells which may explain why these type of symptoms manifest more often and severely in male children. Some studies of human brains show that the neurons in the frontal lobe of neurotypical individuals are differentiated in structure from other brain cells, while in individuals with autism, the neurons in their frontal lobe are the same as other neurons in the brain, or undifferentiated. In PET scans of

Autism Aspergers: Understanding from the Inside Out

people diagnosed with ADHD, their is little activity in the frontal lobe, while in people without ADHD, the amount of activity and energy use in the frontal lobe is much higher. Maybe that's why normal and routine or redundant activities are experienced as too boring and uncomfortable for the people with low frontal lobe activity- they need more novelty, risk, and excitement to pay attention.

Do you have a child who seems smart but struggles to organize and regulate their behavior or emotions?

Why does this happen?
Often when children fail to meet our expectations we feel frustrated. For example, you ask your child to clean their room, twenty minutes later you check on him and he is playing around and has made no progress. What gives? Or maybe you send her to her room to get her shoes, put them on, and come to the front door because it is time to go to school. Fifteen minutes later, you go to see what happened to her, and she is in her room fooling around with something she

found. Or how about the child who blows up when it is time to turn off the video game?

These children are often viewed as oppositional, defiant, or lazy. What is really going on is they are struggling because they lack the thinking skills to adapt successfully to changes in the environment or organize and regulate goal-directed behavior. These thinking skills are called executive functions. When we ask a child to clean their room and they openly resist or obediently go to their room but don't get the job done, we often conclude they are unmotivated or defiant. We often fail to realize the child who is not getting the room picked up may lack the thinking skills necessary to organize the task. They look at all the stuff in their room, and they don't know where to start. It's not that they won't or don't care, it's that they simply don't know how. The child who does not return to the front door with shoes on may have a weak working memory, again a thinking skill or executive function, and they forget what they are supposed to be doing. The child who blows up when it is time to turn off the video game may have weak skills in flexibility and emotional control.

The good news: these are teachable skills.

What are they?

Inhibition

The ability to filter inappropriate responses and not blurt them out or act on impulse.

Working Memory

This is short-term memory, an average person can hold seven bits or chunks of information in short-term memory, which is why a phone number is seven digits. If working memory is not working well, then the information may not be held long enough to encode it into long term memory, so learning would be impaired. This is what is not working when you tell your kid to get his shoes on because it's time to go, he goes to his room, and doesn't return, and when you go to check they are playing in their room and when they see you it's "Oh, yeah, I forgot."

Metacognition

This is the ability to think about what you are thinking about. Self-awareness is the product, and without it, we have a lack of ability to notice that what we are thinking is wrong or off-topic for the context. Individuals with weak metacognition may be unaware that they daydream even when you ask them. Have you ever said "What were you thinking?" and been answered with "I don't know?" Here's your sign.

Cognitive Flexibility/shift

The ability to shift mental sets. When some of the kids entering their elementary school classroom from recess continue running around and shouting while most are sitting down and engaging with the next routine, those kids who have failed to adjust their behavior to match the new context and continue to act like they are at recess are showing difficulty changing or shifting their mental set.

Emotional Control

The abilty to regulate behavior in the face of and tolerate strong emotions.

Autism Aspergers: Understanding from the Inside Out

Initiation

The ability to get started. Some people have difficulty starting tasks, especially unpleasant ones or unpredictable tasks like calling someone and making a social invitation. Some people overthink and overwhelm themselves. Ready, shoot, aim.

Sustain Attention

Ability to maintain attention and not get distracted. Squirrel!

Organization

Putting things into categories, breaking larger tasks into manageable steps, cleaning a desk or room. Some folks take one look at the mess and don't know where to start and get lost in all the details.

Prioritization

The person who spends so much time choosing a font for their project that they don't get it written in the allotted time is showing trouble with prioritization.

Planning

Ability to think about the future, be ready when it's time to go, use a calendar to schedule events

Neuroplasticity- Grandma in Her Wheelchair

The good news is- if some part of the brain is damaged or fails to develop as expected, another part, with practice and effort, grows to manage a task with ever-increasing fluency. When someone has a stroke, they may become hemiplegic- unable to move half of their body. The part of the brain that controlled that half of the body is dead, and ain't comin' back. What if it was your grandmother, and the physical therapist came to the house or hospital bed to begin rehab, and came out after one try and said, nope, she didn't want to work at it and couldn't do it. Guess we're done here. No way. They come back again, and again, pushing, cajoling, encouraging. With any luck grandma will go from her wheelchair to a walker to a cane and hopefully after months of work walk independently and speak clearly again. This is because some other area of the brain took over that function and organized itself and grew until the behavior- movement- could be performed with greater fluency. We can do the same with all kinds of thinking and behavior skills. Practice, practice, reward, and practice. Never give up.

That's what makes this kind of intervention a hard sell- it's a lot of repetitive work, and none too exciting.

I think that executive skills tend to be overlooked as an intervention, thinking skills that we can remediate or compensate for, because we can teach expected behaviors, but if an individual doesn't have the underlying processing hardware available, they still fall short of doing what is expected and keeping up.

Executive Function Remediation/Compensation Strategies

In general:

Osmosis won't work; teach the skills

Keep in mind the concept of plasticity, the brains ability, through effort, positive reinforcement, and coaching to form new connections and even generate new neurons to create abilities that are not currently present. A good example of what happens in any kind of therapy is the stroke patient who loses the ability to move half of her body due to damage in the brain. In physical therapy, she is encouraged to work and move and progresses from the wheelchair to a walker to a cane to walking unassisted. New parts of the brain can develop and assume functions with time and effort. (The Brain That Changes Itself, by Norman Doidge, MD, 2007).

Observation- Watch for situations and specific information about when they are successful and when they are not.

Modify tasks to match current abilities, for example, study for 15 minutes if that is about how long you can study before getting distracted.

Use incentives- set yourself up with first-then to gradually build skills, for example, first I will plan my homework schedule or study for 17 minutes, then I will call my friends for Frisbee in the park.

Set up practice trials

Provide only as much support as needed

Gradually remove supports- scaffolding

Be aware that the first skills to go when under stress are the weakest "links," make a plan to manage stress, exercise often, sleep regular hours, take a brief nap in the day if you can, schedule fun and "down" time but avoid late night parties.

Modify the environment- Remember the ABC's
- Antecedent, what comes before the behavior, for example, if you notice that when you stay up late the next morning you are more distracted, stop staying up late, if you notice you can focus after exercising, exercise before doing homework. Create a regular time and place to plan and study. Set alarms or appointment reminders on phone or computer to support self-monitoring and staying on schedule. Notice if you study best sitting up, laying down, on the bed, the floor, with the TV on or off, in a public or private place, with natural or artificial lighting, with or without a snack.

- Behavior, what you watch to determine if your plan is working

- Consequence- manipulate what comes after successful efforts to reward

- Inhibit- practice and reward not giving in to impulses such as interruptions or responding to provocations from siblings or peers. Build the skill. For young children, make them earn things so they learn to delay gratification, help them understand there are consequences (natural or supplied by you) for poor self-control, prepare them for situations requiring them to wait, practice in role play.

- Working memory- make lists, activity schedule, text messages, picture board, practice digits backwards, take notes, draw pictures symbolizing intentions and concepts, teach rehearsal (subvocalizing) and memorization strategies, palm pilot, day planner, vibrating alarm. Have a child repeat over and over in a chant or sing-song as they are embarking on a task "Go to my room, find my shoes, put them on, come to the front door." Practice daily repeating digits, starting where they are fluent, like "I'm going to say some numbers, and I want you to say them back to me, 3, 4, 9." When they get good at repeating seven digits, start back at two or three but have them say the digits back to you backwards (9, 4, 3).

- Emotional control- The Incredible 5-point Scale, by Buron and Curtis, 1993; to grade and build earlier awareness that an emotional response is occurring, relaxation strategies such as meditation, activity tools such as anything fun or exercise, social tools) talking to someone you trust), thinking tools- grade the size of the problem on a scale from 1-10, systematic desensitization by imagining the feared outcome and then practicing relaxation to train the body to relax in the face of stressful stimuli. Make a chart that includes triggers to angry or worried feelings, things you may want to do but can't, and good things to do with upset feelings, how to be mad the right way, what to do or think to help yourself feel better, then practice daily in role-play. Remind and reward generously when triggers occur to encourage practice "in real life."

- Sustained attention- set up a visual time-timer www.timetimer.com, self monitoring tape www.addwarehouse.com, this site also has programmable vibrating alarms you can set at irregular intervals to remind you to check if you are on task, incentives, praise, reduce distractions, follow a schedule and create a space for homework, healthy breaks.

- Task Initiation- just do the first problem (trick yourself into starting, then you may do one more), do it now instead of later, visual cues, make a schedule, reinforce for timeliness, set alarms, have child make schedule and define how cues will be given, make a list and prioritize, get a coach to text/IM several times a week to monitor progress.

- Planning/Prioritization- Person Centered Plan, break into smaller steps, help child make a schedule, use things you/they really want as rewards when steps are completed, schedule planning time daily as well as times to check progress on plan and mark out completed tasks, get a buddy to talk it out with and take notes.

- Organization- Put a system in place and monitor for fidelity, don't put it down; put it away, make labels or pictures to show what goes where, make pictures of how it should look, make a space for everything that is clearly marked, schedule a time to organize, make a checklist for routines and for the steps of cleaning a room that the child can interact with by checking off steps or moving pictures of steps arranged in sequence from "Now" position to a "done" box.

- Time management- use schedules, calendars, and alarms www.watchminder.com, write down estimates of how long each step in a task will take and record results to learn if you need to adjust how long things will take, schedule and plan for breaks, minimize distractions.

- Flexibility- learn to watch out for absolute or extreme forms of thinking errors and correct the thoughts, keep an eye out for words in your self-talk such as never, always, have to, and can't. Make a game with extreme statements (I always miss, I never get it right, you never let me do anything) made by a person when a disappointing or unexpected event occurs. Have the child generate smarter and more accurate self-talk (I missed this time but if I keep trying I will get it.)

• Metacognition- learn to ask yourself questions such as What am I thinking about, is what I am doing working, what is another way to do this, how do I know when I am finished, keep a journal of thoughts that distract you or occur when you are having an emotional response. Prompt a child to evaluate their own performance- "How do you think you did?" Ask them to predict how their actions may make others feel. Teach them to listen first and use comments to find out more about others rather than lecturing or correcting others, practice at the dinner table.

• Goal-directed persistence- Start easy and build. Use tasks the child enjoys, like increasingly difficult lego building projects. Chart progress so they can see how they are getting better at working longer. Allow them to earn money for chores and set up a savings program for something big they really want.

• Self-Other Awareness- Use video, play back to the student and help them identify all the things they did well in terms of prosocial behavior and effective communication, then help them pick one thing they would like to work on during the next video of interaction, which can be with peers or with a coach such as in Interpersonal Recall Therapy conducted by some speech pathologists. Use video and pause on frames that hold an expression on another's face and ask what could this mean, what is this person thinking, who are they having these thoughts about, what could be the consequences for you if you continue this behavior. Develop a self-monitoring sheet with numerous boxes for different times during the day, have the student check if they are on task and "x" if they are not, provide graduated rewards based not on the number of times on task but number of times they noticed if they were or were not.

Keep in mind that if inhibition or working memory are poorly developed, these must be targeted first, as subsequent organizational and self-control strategies are unlikely to take root until these are addressed.

Try googling "Mind Up" to see the executive skills curriculum that has been legislated as mandatory for public schools in several states. Google "Tools of the Mind" to see research and techniques involving an executive skills curriculum- this has been piloted in many school districts with huge successes- the kids who did the executive skills curriculum instead of the academic curriculum dramatically outperformed their control group peers in the standardized academic testing at the end of their school years.

This is part of what makes socializing so difficult- you need to think about what you want to say as well as consider what others are saying and you need to watch their reactions to you all at the same time.

Autism Aspergers: Understanding from the Inside Out

Communication

Thinking in pictures vs thinking in words

When I'm doing a live workshop I like to ask people "What are your thoughts?" Then I get more specific- "I mean, are your thoughts pictures or words, when you think, is it like a movie in your mind, or more like just feeling, or is it talking in your head, and if it's talking, whose voice is it? Do you have conversations with other people in your head when you think, do you combine this with feelings and images?" So if you are thinking in pictures or a video stream, how do you step outside your video to make another video to analyze the first video- in other words, how do you think about what you are thinking about to analyze how reasonable your thoughts are and if your thinking about what you intend to think about or are supposed to think about? If you are thinking in words, you can do this, you can think to yourself, "That makes me mad, I'd like to kick her- whoops, no, I better not, that would be mean, and I could get in trouble." See, wala! We have self-monitor and inhibition skills! Language in the form of words make this possible, words are a shortcut. If I am thinking in words, it's easy for me to say those words to someone else and they will probably understand what I am trying to represent with the words. But I can't upload a video from my head to yours. Remember those primitive TRS80 computers that came out in the early 80's? The first games, like Gilgamesh's Tavern, they were script, or words running down the screen. Then we started using games with more graphics, and we needed a LOT more processing power and memory. It may be like this for our brains, too, thinking in words only uses a little capacity, pictures or graphics take a lot more. Words are a shortcut that bridge understanding from me to you. What if I was trying to communicate to you with pictures and we didn't share a common lexicon?

Engineers tend to say they think in pictures, teachers, in words, and when a word-thinker hears that there are those who think not in words, but pictures, they often are flabbergasted, taken aback, and have a hard time bending their mind around this alien thought form.

Autism Aspergers: Understanding from the Inside Out

An engineer can look at something and instantly grasp how it works or how to put it together. What happens when they try to explain it? They get frustrated, because it's so obvious to them, it's right there in plain sight, but finding the words for the picture-thinker to explain it to the word-thinker is a daunting task. Two different languages. Mac and PC.

We use self talk or inner language to regulate emotions and problem solve.

This is why I encourage the use of visual supports- they don't need to be fancy, like drawing stick figures with thought and word bubbles to convey a message about social expectations and outcomes, because often people on the spectrum have difficulty forming concepts that words are meant to represent. Put it in a visual to help build understanding and use as a prompt or reminder again later in a teachable moment. When we see repetitive behaviors this often signals that the child's brain is unable to assimilate the perceptual patterns into a meaningful whole, so they are stuck repeating, this also explains how some kids can repeat the sound patterns of a passage they read or video they heard but are unable to answer comprehension questions about what they have memorized. They have the pattern but not the concepts that are symbolized. Also when they are in an environment that becomes non-meaningful they may engage in repetitive and even disruptive behaviors such as shrieking, they are trying to create a pattern they know to drown out the nonsense, which could be the background noise of other people quietly talking or an air conditioner running.

How do you teach someone to begin using their inner language to self-regulate and problem-solve, to become a more fluent user of word-based language? You can narrate what they are doing as they do it- "Oh, now you are trying to make the blue one balance on top of the yellow block." You can narrate your own experience, and do your thinking out loud, "Hmm, well this key is not unlocking the door. I could try and force it but it might break. Let me try one of the other keys to see if it works better." Finally, get the child to re-state a word problem out loud and in their own words, and talk their way out loud through possible paths to solutions. "So, you have 11 apples to start, and you take away 3 because 2 are given away and you eat one, so... that would be like 11-3, I'm supposed to say how many are left, that would be 8 apples left.

Pragmatics is the use of language in social situations. A person can have a highly developed vocabulary and still not communicate effectively with others. Social skills groups and speech therapy in small groups can help.

Research indicates that only 7% of a person's message is communicated by the words they say- the other 93% of the message is conveyed by nonverbal cues such as tone, expression, and body posture. Try playing charade games that require the use and interpretation of nonverbal communication only. There are several Cranium games that incorporate charades, sculpting, and drawing to guess a word, such as Cranium Conga, which is perfect, because it is a "guess what I am thinking" game, which is exactly what we want our kids to be in the habit of doing when they share space with others- to monitor them closely at all times for clues- mostly nonverbal- about what they are thinking and planning.

Autism Aspergers: Understanding from the Inside Out

Sensory Issues

Many people with autism have trouble organizing sensory input into meaningful categories and packets. Proprioception is how you determine where you are in relation to other objects such as the wall, the floor, and other people. If you are seated right now your brain coordinates and makes sense of what you feel through your seat, your feet, your back, information about balance from your inner ear, and information from your eyes to help you know you are safely seated, not too close or far relative to others, and you are safe- not at risk of falling. Someone with disrupted proprioception either isn't getting all the sensory data into their brain or their brain isn't making consistent sense of the data for the individual to know they are safe and not at risk for falling. So this person may start seeking more information- by bouncing in their seat to get more data pushing up into their brains from their backsides, or touching the floor or others around them, or sitting on a leg since this compresses the knee joint which is full of nerve endings.

When seated on the floor some of these children may roll around and touch others repeatedly after being prompted to sit still and keep hands to self. When walking down the hall they drag a hand on the wall, if you make them withdraw the hand, then they have trouble walking straight in the line and may zigzag from wall to wall- because their balance and vision are not enough to keep them oriented to the correct distance from other people and the right side wall in the hall. Some kids with sensory issues may start getting anxious about going to school, not be able to communicate why, and even refuse to go. Others may act out at school or come home hyperactive and crashing around as a result of sensory dis-integration and overload.

What do you do? Put them in a beanbag chair or seat them on a deep soft cushion or put a lap weight or weighted vest on them. Send them out for some running around and joint compressions. Brush by the Wilbarger protocol (google it if

Autism Aspergers: Understanding from the Inside Out

you are not familiar with this technique). Send them for occupational therapy to remediate the problem as much as possible. You can schedule breaks in the school day for downtime, and in schools that have an OT sensory room in place, I've seen kids get to do their breaks here and get themselves the kind of sensory input they need to become organized and focus again. Sometimes we call this a "sensory diet," we schedule activities such as swinging or jumping on a little trampoline at regular times during the day to prevent the overload and acting out before it happens. We can also assign what are known as "heavy work activites," you can see several lists of these posted in Forms4u under the same title. Another effective intervention is to find out what is unpleasant and overwhelming and avoid the trigger, like warning them and keeping them out of fire drills.

One time I was in an ARD/IEP meeting for an elementary student who had not eaten his lunch in 6 months, because the noise in the cafeteria was just too much for him. The principal said, "Well, he's got to learn to get used to the cafeteria sometime." Really? How has not eating lunch impacted the child's learning, their physical and mental health? I don't eat in cafeterias because I don't like them, this has not caused me any problems. There's nothing wrong with accommodating the student and letting them eat somewhere else, for pete's sake.

Autism Aspergers: Understanding from the Inside Out

Student Interviews- What's hard, What Helped?

When I interviewed these students they identified stress and fitting in with peers as the two most important factors to manage in achieving success and a modicum of comfort in school and life.

Here is a list of what they said they had trouble with and what helped:

<u>What was hard</u>

trouble being with so many kids in one classroom

trouble staying on topic

people said I was gay in third grade

trouble starting conversations

asking questions and being shut out

correcting others- I bet they get corrected often so they think that's how to interact

getting bullied- even in kindergarten, teacher didn't help

can't remember names

have no idea why they get picked on

get stressed out easily

special ed teachers focusing too much on the disorder and what's wrong

What helped

need a place to hide or get away from everybody for awhile

learning not to ruminate on injustices

I made a commitment- don't be miserable this year- I wound up making a few friends

finding ways to let stress out

engaging in pleasureful activities

earplugs

unschool- taking a break from school for a year

testing for learning style and matching learning activities

Autism Aspergers: Understanding from the Inside Out

Functional Implications: Disrupted Sensory Processing

How overwhelming is a kinder room? The noise, the number of people, all the stuff on the walls, where can they go to escape and recharge? I would suggest that a reasonable accommodation would be to provide a couple of breaks during the day in a very low-stim environment- cut some windows in a dishwasher box and let the student decorate it as a private "office" where they can crash on a beanbag chair and wrap up in a snuggly blanket. Some people are unable to eat in a noisy, crowded cafeteria. So they get in trouble mostly in music class? Put a chair or desk just outside the room where they can get away but still be seen or give them some earplugs/headphones/earmuffs. It can be hard to know when to push a kid to get them used to something, and when to relent, but in a situation like they are not eating lunch for months or they are becoming aggressive I think the answer should be pretty clear. Let them eat someplace else.

Self-esteem

How often do they get ranked at the bottom socially or in academics, how often do they get negative or corrective feedback vs. praise and support?

Praising for how smart they are has pitfalls- avoidance of anything they may not do great at, so try to praise perseverance and grit instead. Wanting to be the best every time can create dis-ease with the self when it doesn't happen, so focus on praising reasonable effort and perseverance. Recent research on self-esteem indicates that a lot of our satisfaction or lack thereof comes from ranking- we constantly compare ourselves to others, so get them really good at something. You can get them private lessons and create practice opportunities for something they have passion and talent for.

I hope you had at least one person you knew growing up who influenced you to think of yourself in positive and encouraging ways. In middle school I had an English teacher, Billie

Autism Aspergers: Understanding from the Inside Out

Hoffman, whose eyes crinkled and twinkled smilingly even when someone displayed inappropriate behavior. One time she overheard a classmate use a word that doesn't belong in the classroom. She smiled and had the student pull a chair up to her desk along with the other students who were within earshot, smiled even more broadly, like always, and said, "Why don't you tell us what you think that means, Bob?" She could always defuse and redirect with her quiet humor and ever-smiling face. She never needed to get mad, show frustration, offer criticism, or judge. Somehow just knowing that she was seeing you and knowing you had goodness and the capacity to do better made her able to handle any sort of problem in her classroom. She had mastered the art of something very valuable- she learned to *see what the kids could be not just what they are not.* What sort of contributions might their uniqueness create? Billie Hoffman never lowered herself to use fear, threats, or the pain of punishment to maintain order in our space.

Along the way there were a few others who inspired me to become my best self. These were all people who loved the power of love more than they loved power.

My intention with this paragraph is to give you permission to become the person who can influence people with the power of love, encouragement, and positive regard like a few great masters influenced me. Be wary of looking at a person as a problem to be solved. Children want an opportunity to engage in making the world; they are made stronger when their voices and abilities are recognized.

Tunnel Vision

Preoccupation with details, lacking central coherence and the ability to get the big picture, can be a problematic characteristic of autism. Frequent reminders to step back and ask "What is this really about," and "What does this person want from me" can make this kind of thinking more automatic. Developing special interests may help create an experience of central coherence and help develop an identity. What would it be like if you tried to drive into a city, and you couldn't not get caught up in the details of what it said on every billboard, rather than having a brain that easily detaches from non-salient details and can stay focused on what is relevant to your intentions and safety? It wouldn't feel very safe.

Social Skills

Difficulty reading the context and knowing how rules change with different places and people can interfere with social success. Remember they are little and consider their media consumption- what if they imitate what they are absorbing? Aggression/ aggressive style of dealing with conflict is a common characteristic of video games and television. Some kids are just better off not being exposed to the fear-pandering news media and frightening/aggressive viewing content. Garbage in, garbage out, so carefully monitor and manage what is going into your kids' brain.

Social skills take time and effort to develop, which is why I have a video soley devoted to teaching social skills to children aged 4-8 (a great video at www.icyouvideo.com). In the resources section at the end of this book, you will find a list of resources; games, books, and curricula, that I have found useful in my practice conducting social skills groups which I have done for over 15 years.

Autism Aspergers: Understanding from the Inside Out

The most important things that I learned follow.

1. You have to get buy-in. This means you must create an experience in which it is more fun and exciting being in the group than it is to be alone. If you have a person who doesn't want to be in the group and doesn't want to work on social skills, your job is going to be much more difficult.

2. Birds of a feather flock together. A child who is spectrum-ish may do better and feel more comfortable befriending other children who are quirky in similar ways. Think Big Bang Theory.

3. All the social skills work and therapy in the world may not result in making someone who stands out as being a little different blend in perfectly with neurotypicals. Instead, target embracing the differences and celebrating strengths. When a person is comfortable with themselves, can acknowledge and laugh about their idiosynchrasies, and doesn't get all nervous and weird about themselves in a group, they can

be found by others very likable and personable; this ability is more important in relationships than perfect social skills.

Autism Aspergers: Understanding from the Inside Out

Problem Solving

Trouble recognizing that there may be many ways to solve the same problem, the brain on autism may try one way and then have difficulty adapting and trying another way if it doesn't work, it may get stuck or fall apart here, tend not to use internal dialogue or self-talk to problem solve. We can teach talking out and generating multiple solutions through narration and modeling; narrate their efforts and think out loud in their presence when you are solving a problem.

Use the "problem-solving template" in Forms4u to reinforce the idea that their are many possible solutions to try for the same problem.

They may exhibit "Frank Sinatra syndrome"- I want it my way position on all interpersonal problems, or at least especially when they get emotionally involved.

Comorbid Mood Disorder

About 65% of people with autism spectrum disorder have a comorbid mood disorder according to Tony Attwood, so it's more the rule than the exception. Be ready to seek help if needed in treating concurrent mental health issues if they develop. Any mention of killing themselves should receive professional attention.

Extreme Emotional Response

Emotional response may be either excessive or lacking. Typically a child with autism spectrum disorder may be 3 years behind in emotional development, so if an 8 year old tantrums like a 5 year old, this is not unexpected. They may tend not to grade feelings or distinguish a range and gradation of feelings- either calm or top of the scale angry. If they are having major meltdowns daily or several times a week, I suggest dramatically cutting back expectations until they return to their emotional baseline, teach them skills for frustration tolerance, build self-esteem through success, and then gradually add the expectations back in. An example would be rewarding for just being at school without becoming disruptive and without any work requirements, then slowly add some work requests as part of how they earn their rewards. Help them develop an emotional vocabulary- use numbers and pictures to represent levels of intensity for the emotion, like 1 is calm, 2 is annoyed, 3 is frustrated, 4 is mad, 5 is furious. Have them make their own pictures or faces to go with the levels. I've also used animals and weather patterns, etc, like 1 is a sunny day, 2 a cloudy day, 3 rain, 4 storm, 5 tornado. To see this process in greater detail see my video Anger and Children and/or Anxiety and Children at www.ICYouvideo.com.

I think it's important for people to both recognize and convey their feelings, and it sure is prettier if it comes out in words instead of behavior! A person who is exhibiting emotional excess needs to know not only what they can't do, but what they can do when upset, they need a way to signal or communicate when they need help, a break, or to use a coping skill.

Brenda Smith Myles came up with a neat way to facilitate this process- the powercard. I use this sometimes in my office, first they pick a favorite hero, we select an image on the computer and print it pocket-sized, and put a social story about what the hero does when they are mad on the back. Then the kids can show their card to signal they are upset and needing a break

Autism Aspergers: Understanding from the Inside Out

or a distraction. Here's an example an eight year old made in a social skills group about his superhero Hawkeye:

When Hawkeye is hanging out with other people at home or in the community, people sometimes say things that he doesn't like. They might tell him "No," or say something a little mean or hurtful. Usually other people are not trying to hurt anybody's feelings. When Hawkeye is upset at first he may want to run away or pierce them with an arrow, but that would be an overreaction that would surprise, confuse, or even scare other people. Hawkeye knows he needs to have a small reaction to small problems and use his words to say how he feels and ask for what he wants- "That bothers me I wish you would_____." Hawkeye has a hard time controlling his reactions and he will try to use his words and not yell, run away, or shoot people for saying things he doesn't like. Then other people will know how he feels and what he wants, and they will feel more comfortable being around him.

Defense Mechanisms

These defense mechanisms illustrate the importance of treating someone who is struggling with support, encouragement, and compassion. Feeling rejected, judged, and criticized engenders tendencies to rebel and resist or withdraw and give up.

Reactive depression- overly apologetic, self-critical, withdrawn, says "I don't know" often, troubled eating and sleeping patterns.

Escape into imagination- I'm an Indian, and Indians don't have to go to school. If life hurts too much just make up a new one, intense interest in another culture or time zone, another country, world of animals, video games, pretending to be an animal. Usually a dog, cat, or hamster.

Autism Aspergers: Understanding from the Inside Out

Denial and arrogance- God mode, may misinterpret the intentions of others like if they lose, it was because someone cheated or made them lose on purpose as an act of aggression, righteous indignation, make good lawyers, make arguments you can't win and they pull you in. Need to be right and need others agreement, may try and make others agree with them even if physical force and hurting them is necessary.

Imitation- Can mimic another perfectly, speaking in scripts, enjoy being on the stage when playing a defined role, I once knew a twin who watched Aladdin when he was little and spoke just like Iago the parrot- Gilbert Gottfried 24/7 for many years afterwards. He had it down perfect, too. His brother used his own voice.

Concluding Comments (What they said)

Remember they are people too, people who are a little different but not all that different from you.

Consider modifying their environment to help them avoid stress and meet their needs.

Focus on interests and learning and developing a passion rather than taking a test and don't make it all just work, work, work.

"I hope nobody has to go through what I did: Everyone should have someone they can rely on, that they can trust." Find them someone at school they can rely on and trust.

Medicines may have side effects.

What would their ideal school look like?

Autism Aspergers: Understanding from the Inside Out

My Concluding Comments

Remember that love and happiness are acts of faith, courage, and discipline.

Faith is when you choose to believe in something even if direct evidence has not yet supported your belief. This is a belief you have committed to and don't look back on. Like believing that the kid you care about is going to be okay, they will learn and change, they will adjust and adapt, you don't know when they will have their successes but you will be there patient and smiling when it starts to happen. Take this action to heart, make your leap of faith if you haven't already, and your child will be able to interpret it from the nature of your posture, tone, and words with them. Do not give in to fear, as whichever path you choose; fear, criticism, and judgement, or faith, love, and support, you will be leading them right there with you.

Courage means you keep going even when you are afraid, that you remain steadfast in your thinking and your behavior in the pursuit of your goals and values.

Discipline is taking personal responsibility for your thoughts, your feelings, your behavior, your life, and the changes you want. These changes start with your thoughts and feelings, your practice of mastering your state of being. There is no waiting or blaming, this is the life you have, this is the one and only moment you live in, right now, work hard and be willing to do that which may at first feel uncomfortable for you in the pursuit of a prioritized life.

The reason I detailed the difficulties someone on the spectrum is expected to have is to promote understanding, effective interventions, and most especially to address a pet peeve of mine. I do not like it when a person is judged and labeled as making "bad choices" or having a defective character when they in fact lack the confidence and thinking skills they need to adapt successfully to the demands of the environment. This type of judging is demoralizing, devaluing, and doesn't help anyone do better.

I want you to become that person for someone else that always has compassion, always thinks well of them, continues to encourage and support even when unexpected behaviors are occurring. Hopefully you had at least one person in your life who you knew always saw you as your highest self. You realize how powerful you can be by allowing yourself to be completely loving. if you can remember someone you knew in your past who influenced you with the gift of unconditional positive regard, you can see and feel how their loving influence has stayed with you through years after the gift was given. These masters of positive influence shared the most valuable thing they had to offer- themselves. Likewise realize the most valuable thing you have to offer is not the ability to understand a variety of complex intervention strategies and resources, the most value you can add to a person who struggles is yourself, your positive, loving, supportive regard and encouragement. Discipline yourself not to give in to fear, criticism, or judgment when you interact with this person, project your positive regard into your voice tone, your words, your body posture, your facial expression, and you will give them a gift that keeps on giving. Sew and you shall reap. Be careful and intentional about what kind of seeds you are planting, and know you are imparting a lasting gift that stays inside the person, comforts them in times of stress, dismay, and doubt, elevates the way they think about themselves.

Resources

Attwood, T. (2007). The Complete Guide to Asperger Syndrome. London: Jessica Kingsley Publishers. <This really is a complete guide by one of the foremost experts in the world on this topic>

Nathaniel R. Riggs, Laudan B. Jahromi, Rachel P. Razza, Janean E. Dilworth-Bart, Ulrich Mueller. Journal of Applied Developmental Psychology. (2006). Jul-Aug; 27(4), p. 300-309

Schonfeld AM, Paley B, Frankel F, O'Connor MJ. Child Neuropsychology. (2006). Dec; 12(6) 439-52 Relationships Between Executive Functions and Language Variables. Suzanne Hungerford, Ph.D., CCC-SLP. &. Katherine Gonyo, M.C.D., CCC-SLP. Language ...
convention.asha.org/2007/handouts/1137_1011Hungerford

Myles, B. & Southwick, J. (2005). Asperger Syndrome and Difficult Moments. Shawnee Mission, Kansas: Autism Asperger Publishing Co. www.asperger.net <Great resource if you are suffering meltdowns>

Grandin, T. (2006). Thinking in Pictures. New York: Vintage Books. <Brilliant book, great read, not sure everyone who has autism thinks just like the author but definitely worth reading>

Social Skills and Social Thinking Curriculum

Gutstein, S. (2002). Relationship Development Intervention with Young Children. London: Jessica Kingsley Publishers. <Great active fun games for younger children to learn to enjoy play!>

Howlin, P., Baron-Cohen, S., Hadwin, J. (2002). Teaching Children with Autism to Mind-Read. West Sussex, England:

Autism Aspergers: Understanding from the Inside Out John Wiley & Sons Ltd. <Curriculum to help children understand desire-based emotion, situation-based emotions, false belief, and perspectives of others>

Madrigal, S., Winner, M. (2008) <u>Superflex... A Superhero Social Thinking Curriculum</u>. San Jose, CA: Think Social Publishing, Inc. <This would be my top recommended curriculum for teaching flexible social thinking skills>

Walker, H., McConnel, S., Holmes, D., Todis, B., Walker, J., and N. Golden. (1983) <u>The Walker Social Skills Program</u>. Austin, TX: Pro-Ed.
<One of the few programs out there with empirical support, involves video, role-play, and behavioral coaching/management of skills taught outside of the social skills teaching place>

Winner, M. (2002). Thinking About You Thinking About Me. San Jose, California: Michelle Garcia-Winner, SLP www.soicalthinking.com <Heavy reading but will help you understand how these kids think>

Winner, M. (2005). Worksheets! For Teaching Social Thinking and Related Skills. San Jose, California: Michelle Garcia Winner, SLP <Great especially if you have lots of skills to teach all school year long>

Winner, M. (2005). Think Social. San Jose, California: Michelle Garcia Winner, SLP <Great especially if you have lots of skills to teach all school year long>

Winner, M. (2008). A Politically Incorrect Look at Evidence-based practices and Teaching Social Skills. San Jose, CA: Think Social Publishing, Inc. <If you want to get into the

Autism Aspergers: Understanding from the Inside Out

arguments about if it's appropriate to use educational resources to teach social skills and explore if teaching social skills can work, this is for you>

Winner, M. (2008) <u>You Are A Social Detective</u>. San Jose, CA: Think Social Publishing, Inc.<A must for younger children who don't understand about keeping their bodies and minds in the group>

Social Group Participation and Health Links

Jetten, J., Haslam, C., Haslam, S., and Nyla Branscombe (2009) Scientific American Mind. Sept/Oct 2009 20(5). Scientific American, Inc. pp. 26-33. <Turns out withdrawal is not good for your health and being in groups is>

Putnam, R.. (2000). Bowling Alone: The Collapse and Revival of American Community. Simon & Schuster.

Cognitive-Behavioral Strategies for Higher Functioning People with Social Learning Disabilities and Self-Regulation Problems

Attwood, T. (2004) <u>Exploring Feelings</u>. Future Horizons, Inc., Arlington, Texas. <Great workbooks that teach skills for managing anger and anxiety>

Attwood, T. (2008). <u>The CAT-Kit</u>. Future Horizons, Arlington, Texas. <Therapist tool for teaching emotional regulation skills>

Avery, R. (2008) <u>Meet Thotso, Your Thought Maker</u>. Smart Thot, LLC. <Teaches younger children the idea of making band-aid thoughts for your boo-boo thoughts to help yourself feel better>

Autism Aspergers: Understanding from the Inside Out

Buron, K. D., & Curtis, M. (2003) <u>The Incredible 1-5 Scale</u>. Shawnee Mission, KS: Autism Asperger Publishing Company.<Terrific technique for mapping out the gradations in an emotional response and develop emotional awareness and coping>

Buron, K. D. <u>A "5" Could Make Me Lose Control</u>! Autism Asperger Publishing Company, Shawnee Mission, KS. www.asperger.net

Gray, C. (1994) <u>Comic Strip Conversations</u>. Future Horizons Publishers: Arlington, Texas www.futurehorizons.com <Neat way to visually teach appropriate language and prediction of perspective and emotion>

Games to Help Build Skillls

Land of Psymon (8-up) Western Psychological Services <This game teaches categories of thinking errors such as extremism, and teaches how to catch unwanted and inaccurate thoughts to replace them with smarter ways to think that also feel better>

My First Therapy Game (6-12) Childtherapytoys.com <Good for stimulating conversation and as an ice-breaker>

Escape From Anger Island (6-12) Instant Help Publications <Strategies for anger>

Ungame www.talicor.com <Any age up to 18, facilitates getting to know one another>

The Talking, Feeling, and Doing Game (4-15) Creative Therapeutics <May help broaden and deepen concepts

around what feelings are and how they can be predicted by context>

Gameskidsplay.net <Tons of outdoor games to help build speed of processing and cooperation>

Fib or Not (10-up) Gather Around Games, Inc. <Using and interpreting affect, understanding deception; an important real world skill>

Hullabalu (4-up) Cranium, Inc. <Great for young kids, learning to follow directions>

Too Much, Too Little, Just Right (5-12) Creative Therapy Store <Helps to teach skills to discriminate the appropriate size of a reaction, amount of volume, degree of animation>

Imaginiff (10-up) Crystal Lines <Great for teaching thinking about others skills>

Moods-(teen/adult) Hasbro <Build affective and emotional intelligence/vocabulary>

Kid Cranium SpongeBob (7-up) Hasbro <All these Cranium games help develop communication, especially nonverbal communication skills>

Any charade game is good too!

Autism Aspergers: Understanding from the Inside Out

Appendix

Why Autism?

One of the questions I am most often asked is why is the prevalence of autism so much on the rise? How could we go from 4 in 10,000 to 1 in 100? I believe the rise in autism in our country sends us some very clear and important messages- about ourselves. First, we are being led down the path of exploring what it means to be human in a social context, that is, how we are supposed to behave and think in relationship to other people. It is a journey with the potential for us to define and reshape who we are and how we want to be. It is an opportunity to challenge cultural trends that encourage egocentrism, or thinking only about ourselves, trends that encourage anxiety and the drive to always want more and better.

In other cultures and ancient history children with neurological disorders became shamans. They were allowed to live away from the group and be different. They were cared for in terms of food in daily living and their unique thinking styles and abilities contributed to the welfare of the group. There was no effort to make different people the same as everybody else as we do now in Western culture and educational institutions. We try to make different people over in the image our culture says people should be, adhering to rigid and abstract standards, ignoring reality. I call this the autism of the system.

We can learn to be people who think about others, we can learn how to accept ourselves as we are rather than always feeling as though we must have more, we must increase our possessions and wealth, we must always be getting something to improve our status or we are not worthy. WE could learn to be more flexible and accepting.

From an evolutionary perspective, perhaps nature or God throws out individuals that are extremely different from time to time, may be sometimes it works out. And sometimes it doesn't. But look at Edison, how different he was, his difficulty socializing during school as a child and then the contributions he brought back. Where do you think rocket ships, computers, and electric light came from?

Finally, these children may be serving as another type of early warning system. Their heightened sensitivities to toxic byproducts of modern industrialization and current mass agriculture practices and the degradation of our food may be predictive of what we all have in store for us if we don't read the signs and change our habits. We must take care of our planet and take care of ourselves. This is the message they bring, a warning and a signpost to better mental and physical health practices, a better society and culture. It is a message we are sending to ourselves.

Signs of Asperger Syndrome

Asperger Syndrome or AS has been removed as a clinical category of "mental disorder" from the DSM V, which means it is no longer a clinical diagnostic category with a corresponding code that can be used to get reimbursement for therapy and treatment. However, since somewhere around a million people in the US alone consider themselves "Aspies," and this is a population that resists change, the term is unlikely to drop from our common vernacular anytime soon. AS is characterized by difficulties in social interaction and narrow or restricted patterns of interest. This may include failure to use eye contact, develop peer relationships, and share enjoyment with others as expected. You may also see preoccupation with parts of objects, intense focus on a particular subject such as dinosaurs, Pokemon, a video game, weather, or Thomas the Train, inflexibility in routines, and repeated motor mannerisms. Some people have some of the characteristics but not all, and may be diagnosed as PDD-NOS, ADHD, OCD, or Bipolar.

Social anxiety and difficulty recognizing, communicating, and managing emotional responses are also frequently seen in this population. Many of these people are socially interested and have good intentions and are at times very sensitive, yet lack the cognitive flexibility and social communication and thinking skills necessary to navigate the social world gracefully.

They often seem unaware of unwritten social rules until explicitly taught- they don't "get it" as naturally as their neurotypical peers do. Often we see high intelligence and vocabulary, a collector of information on a specific topic of interest, terrific long-term rote memory coupled with difficulty with everyday problem-solving skills. They may neglect to develop social curiosity about what other people are thinking, failing to realize that other people have a

Autism Aspergers: Understanding from the Inside Out

different mind with different interpretations, intentions, and feelings- they may seem only aware of one mind, their own.

Language may be atypical, with unusual pitch, volume, prosody, and/or rhythym. You may hear monotone, sing-song, or the little professor, "Well, actually…" and then a monlogue ensues that may continue long after the listener has shown signs of disinterest or even left the room! Use of language may be literal and concrete, failing to interpret jokes, idioms, figures of speech. Attempts at entering into groups may be characterized by off-topic remarks or quotes from a favorite video.

Motor skills may be delayed. Difficulty riding a bike, tying shoes, and writing are commonly seen.

Autism Sensitivity Resources

My best friend Will- (child's perspective of having a friend with ASD)

http://www.amazon.com/Best-Friend-Jamie-Lowell-Tuchel/dp/1931282757/ref=sr_1_1?ie=UTF8&qid=1396648238&sr=8-1&keywords=my+best+friend+will

All Cats have Asperger Syndrome- (so great)

http://www.amazon.com/All-Cats-Have-Asperger-Syndrome/dp/1843104814/ref=sr_1_1?ie=UTF8&qid=1396648266&sr=8-1&keywords=all+cats+have+aspergers

Fish is Fish (focuses on the perspective taking aspect of ASD)

http://www.amazon.com/Fish-Leo-Lionni/dp/0394827996/ref=sr_1_1?ie=UTF8&qid=1396648291&sr=8-1&keywords=fish+is+fish

Autism Aspergers: Understanding from the Inside Out

Swimmy- (focus on how differences make us stronger)

http://www.amazon.com/Swimmy-Leo-Lionni/dp/0394826205/ref=sr_1_1?ie=UTF8&qid=1396648306&sr=8-1&keywords=swimmy

Me I am- (focuses on the importance of uniqueness)

http://www.amazon.com/Me-I-Am-Jack-Prelutsky/dp/0374349029/ref=sr_1_1?ie=UTF8&qid=1396648340&sr=8-1&keywords=me+i+am

There is only one you

http://www.amazon.com/Only-One-You-Linda-Kranz/dp/0873589017/ref=sr_1_1?ie=UTF8&qid=1396648322&sr=8-1&keywords=there+is+only+one+you

ABOUT THE AUTHOR

Bradley Keith Mason M.Ed., LSSP, LPC, LPA

Licensed Specialist in School Psychology
Licensed Professional Counselor
Licensed Psychological Associate

Brad Mason has worked in public schools for 12 years as a Special Education Counselor and Licensed Specialist in School Psychology. Prior to that he worked in a brain injury hospital with both adults and children as a Behavior Therapist.

Mr. Mason has been in private practice as a Licensed Professional Counselor for eleven years and operates the Autism Clinic and Family Counseling Center in downtown Georgetown, Texas. He currently works with children, adolescents, adults, and families in groups and individually. He specializes in treating children with social skills deficits and emotional regulation problems. Mr. Mason is the author of the Intensive Care for You video series, available as pay-per-view videos through ICYouvideo.com, created to help leaders of children guide those who struggle in more loving and effective ways.

Mr. Mason has completed a Bachelor's Degree in Psychology and English, a Master's Degree in Education for School Psychology, post-graduate education at St. Edward's University, as well as ongoing education in treating Autism Spectrum Disorders, Family Dynamics, Career Counseling and Advanced Counseling Techniques. Mr. Mason has conducted and published research, in conjunction with various authors, in the fields of aggression, gender role stereotypes, and children's television. Mr. Mason has presented his work for the Southwest Conference on Human Development, and offers presentations and staff development to school districts and various agencies. Frequently provided workshop topics include Social Thinking, Teaching Social Skills Through Play, Behavior Management at it's Best, Relating Effectively to the Oppositional Child, Connecting the Dots and Reaching Children with Asperger Syndrome, HFA, or PDD, Effective Strategies for Managing the Behavior of Children with ADHD, Anxiety and Children, Anger and Children, Prevention and Management of Aggressive Behavior.

Made in the USA
Las Vegas, NV
29 December 2021